THE WAY WE WERE,
THE WAY WE ARE

TED SALVETER III

The Way We Were, The Way We Are

Copyright © 2018 Ted Salveter III

Cover Photo: Theodore Charles Salveter
& Theodore Clifton Salveter
Taken in St. Louis Missouri around 1900

Sharon Kizziah-Holmes, Publishing Coordinator

Paperback-Press
an imprint of A & S Publishing
A & S Holmes, Inc.

ISBN-13: 978-1-945669-71-2

CONTENTS

December 2018

Dear Rachael, Claire & Millie —

I hope you all have a wonderful Christmas. If I keep writing books I may create a complete Galvetes library! Hope you enjoy my latest effort.

Love

PaPa

FOREWORD

My family history may mean nothing to you, or it may mean a great deal. Even someone else's family may be interesting. If you want to study American History, the library is full of books just waiting to be read. There may be books on our family's history, but I am only aware of the three that I wrote: "His Wonderful Life", "The Accidental Lawyer", and "The Fairytale Princess".

I have realized that as each day passes our history fades into the fog of time. In this book I will try to capture as much as I can.

I'm sure that you will be thankful. Someday.

My hope is that my brother Charles Robert Salveter will one day write his own book on these matters. He knows a lot but keeps busy with his tractors and cows. He has demanded that I give no credit to him for any part of this book. Therefore I shall not mention the help he has been with it. Any mistakes or poor penmanship are solely my own. The buck stops here!

CHAPTER ONE

WHAT'S IN A NAME?

I'm not sure that we can nail down exactly what "Salveter" means or where it came from. A long time ago I was mildly curious and did a little research. I came to the conclusion that Salveter comes from the Island of Wales, and therefore we were Welsh. The name derives from a word meaning "Saltmaker" which would make sense since many old names described people's occupations. A Smithy, a carpenter, or a mason, etc. That was good enough for me, and I have ever since proudly declared I was Welsh. From time to time that has been challenged.

So what is it?

Where did our particular family of Salveters come from?

Henry Anthony Salveter is my great grandson. His father is Brennon whose father is Theodore Clifton Salveter IV who in turn is my son. My father is Theodore Clifton Salveter Jr. who is also the father of Charles R. Salveter, Robert Salveter, and Celia Salveter. His father was Theodore Clifton Salveter. His father was Theodore Charles Salveter.

A long time ago Theodore Charles Salveter departed for the Americas from Schleswig-Holstein Germany. A church was established there, and it shows that they came to Germany from Denmark aboard a ship. I suppose they could have been Danish, but I'm not giving up on Welsh just yet. Cousin Pat Warden traces him to Heiligenhafen, Germany near the border with Denmark. Confused? Me too.

How did they get to Missouri?

On the maternal side of my family we have the "Oberhaus". They were mixed with the Tobens of Washington, Missouri, and very German.

My grandfather was Henry Oberhaus and my maternal grandmother was Christine Toben Oberhaus. She died when I was about 12 years old in 1947.

I remember being on a train in 1984 going through the Swiss and German Alps, when suddenly there appeared high on a hill, like at Hollywood California, the town of Oberhausen. That, I thought is where Mom's family had its roots.

My mother, Nelda Marie Anna Oberhaus Salveter, was born on October 10, 1915 in Washington, Missouri and died June 30, 1983 in Springfield, Missouri. She is buried in her family plot in St. Peters Cemetery, Washington, Missouri. My mother had three brothers, Lester Oberhaus, Raymond Oberhaus and Melvin "Bud" Oberhaus. All of Franklin county, Missouri.

So we are either Welsh-German or German-Danish. Or possibly something else.

Charles could straighten this out for sure. However, the name Oberhaus could refer to a habitation, not an occupation, or could refer to a town or location. "Ober" means "upper, above". "Haus, means "house". It could refer to one who came from Oberhaus. Many Oberhaus figure into German history.

Molly Jones Downen

Sharon Downen Salveter's Grandmother, Great Grandmother of Ted IV, Tony and Paige, Great Great Grandmother of Brennon and Rachael and Great Great Great Grandmother of Henry, Clair and Millie.

She homesteaded in the West in the 1800s. Lived in a sod house. Wife of 'Dad Tom' Downen

R. Earl Salveter; Construction Executive

December 19 87 St. Louis

Salveter

A memorial service for R. Earl Salveter, a retired construction company executive, will be held at 3 p.m. Thursday at Webster Groves Presbyterian Church, 45 West Lockwood Avenue in Webster Groves. Burial will be private, in Oakhill Cemetery.

Mr. Salveter died Monday of infirmities at his home in Affton. He was 89.

Mr. Salveter worked in various positions since 1922 with the Woermann Construction Co., 7120 Manchester Road in Maplewood. He was appointed president of the firm in 1951 and retired in 1977. Mr. Salveter graduated from Washington University, where he was a member of the Sigma Chi and Tau Beta Pi fraternities.

His family was one of the first to settle in Webster Groves, and Mr. Salveter served on the city's first city council from 1954 until 1960.

In 1944, Mr. Salveter was elected president of the Master Builders Association of St. Louis. He was a life member and a president of the Engineers Club, a life member of the Civil Engineers Association and a member of the Circle Club of Washington University.

Mr. Salveter was a member of the Webster Groves Presbyterian Church for more than 50 years and had served as an elder and trustee.

Surviving are his wife, Marie Salveter; three sons: R.E. Salveter Jr. of Marion, Ind., Steve Salveter of San Francisco, and Guy Davis of Honolulu, Hawaii; two daughters, Nancy S. Watson of Evansville, Ind., and Angela Davis Burke of Barre, Vt.; 14 grandchildren; and five great-grandchildren.

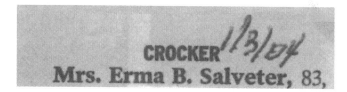

CROCKER 1/3/04

Mrs. Erma B. Salveter, 83,

3

CHAPTER TWO

THIS JOB IS TOO BIG

It's hard enough to get one life straight but a whole family?
Impossible!
But I won't quit.
Theodore Charles Salveter was my great grandfather. We thought for a lot of my life that his middle name was "Clifton" like mine, making me the "IV" not the third. I don't know where Clifton came from. For a while I had IV on my legal stationary which made me look silly when I had to change it. "This guy doesn't even know his own name!"

Theodore Charles was born on the 28th day of September, 1839 in Europe. His parents were Christopher Marcus Salveter and Fredricka Schmidt Salveter. He died on March, 1911 in St. Charles, Missouri. He was a wealthy man. My grandfather was the only boy out of the seven children he had at the time of his death. He lived in the "Salveter Mansion" in St. Charles which is now the Bouie Funeral Home. Great grandpa had four wives, and out lived all of them except the last one. That alone would make you proud of the old boy, but in addition she was only twenty-two and he was fifty-eight when they got married. Way to go great Gramps!

She never remarried and became a recluse in the mansion with her companion. Her name was Eda Meyer Salveter. She lived to a ripe old age and died in 1948 in St. Charles, MO.

When she died my grandpa was appointed administrator of her estate by The Probate Court of St. Charles County. I was only

4

eleven years old. He took me to St. Charles one day to check court and other records. We went to several funeral homes. In one of them I wandered around by myself and went into a parlor with a casket. I walked up to it to give it a look. To my shock and horror there was the body of a dead old woman. I assumed she was dead, but I could have sworn she moved. That was the first dead body I ever saw. I was so scared that I beat a hasty retreat to find "Pop". He wasn't happy about my adventure.

Great grandpa was rich but his widow managed to lose most of it. There wasn't much left by the time she died. Basically just the mansion.

Unbelievably, relatives came from everywhere and cleaned the place out. Didn't want to wait on probate. So when Pop and I got there, there wasn't much left.

It was like the Grinch had taken even the Salveter pudding. The widow was so fearful of the outside world that there were multiple locks on even the interior doors. The place had a two story carriage house which was bigger than the house I grew up in Webster. On the third floor of the house was a ballroom. Nothing was left there either.

I did find a buckeye up there. Pop told me that they were good luck. I carried it for a long time. I guess my luck ran out when I lost it.

By the time the estate was divided up, Pop's share wasn't much and the hope for great riches were gone from our branch.

We could have been contenders!

Great grandpa and all the wives are buried in the St. Charles Cemetery. There is a tall monument with graves all around. The story was that the monument was tilted toward the favorite wife. Those who have looked say it looks pretty straight. Guess he loved them all the same.

So there lies the former president of American Car and Foundry. Wonder how that crowd of women is working out for him now?

How did he get so rich? My recollection was that he did some farming in the Carthage area. No money in that. At some point during the Civil War he was forced to serve in the rebel Arkansas Volunteers. We still have his saber and his Masonic sword. His war experience was brief as he was captured by the Union forces and sat out the war in a Federal concentration camp. His unit did fight in the Battle of Pea Ridge and later in the Oklahoma Territory. It was there that the Confederates tried to get the Indians to fight the Union.

What happened after that?

He made money and invested well in rental and other property in St. Charles County. He was a master carpenter and supervised many big projects as he worked his way up the ladder.

CHAPTER THREE

POP AND MAE B. SALVETER

The oldest relatives I actually knew were my grandparents. Did I really know them? Probably not. Just the tiny part of their lives that involved me, and most of that I have forgotten. Here's what I remember about Theodore and Mae B. Salveter.

As far as I know they were pretty solid people and very refined. I never knew grandma to work, but grandpa had a variety of jobs, mainly in sales.

Bradley was a clothing company that both grandpa and Uncle Charles Wardan traveled for. I still have some of his trunks and other things that he carried his samples around in. Who knows who will end up with things like that? I also remember that grandpa worked for Famous Barr Co. in St. Louis. I believe he was a floor walker.

Back when I was a kid in the 1940's and '50's St. Louis was a large bustling city. Not what it has become. Famous Barr and Stix Bare & Fuller were big department stores downtown. At Christmas time the downtown area was alive with displays in all the windows. People would come from all over with their kids in tow. It was an exciting time. Think of the old movie "Miracle on 34th Street", about Santa and Macy's in New York. That's what it looked like. It was a wonderland to a kid.

Pop had access to all the stuff inside and the magic continued. Santa Claus, Elves, toys galore. Great memories. At the time I thought Pop must be pretty important. I think he was.

Christmas was usually celebrated at their house in Kirkwood or in the hotel they owned and lived in. It was the "Old Oak Manor Hotel" in LeMay. I spent a lot of time with them in both places. Sometimes for days at a time. I was the oldest grandchild. Naturally that made me important.

Charles was 5 years younger. Pat and Randy Wardan my cousins were eight and ten years younger. Celia and Bob Salveter at least 20 years younger than me. I'm sure I did a good job being the oldest. I may have been spoiled a little. However, they expected a lot out of me, and were determined I would learn how to do everything right.

They took me to the Christian Science Church where good morals and ethics were taught. I had to speak right and "to enunciate"! No slurring or soft spoken speech. "Speak up" "Enunciate", "speak distinctly" and "speak correctly". Good manners were emphasized. I needed to know the right fork or spoon to use. To say "thank you" and "please", and to look people in the eye and give them a firm handshake.

I am sure that all of this breeding helped me to be a successful lawyer, teacher and politician. Hopefully it helps me to be a better dad, grandfather, and now great grandfather.

One of my favorite things was to spend the night with them. The teaching never stopped, but we played card games and others too. Before bedtime or during a game of cribbage, canasta, etc. We would have "black cows". To a kid this was a big deal, but it was really just coca cola and ice cream. Grandma Salveter just had chocolate ice cream. Grandma always kissed me good night, but grandpa tucked me in and we discussed God and His place in my life. He always had me say this saying he taught me.

"Today has been as yesterday, and still I stand
The stronger for their passing
Tomorrow I shall meet the day
Confident that God always has met
And always will meet every human need"

I don't know who wrote that, but possibly Mary Baker Eddy. It was a good way to close the day. Sleep came better with those good thoughts to a young boy. Now that I am old I may see things a little differently. I don't get to tuck my kids, grandkids or great grandkids in. Times change. I still want to be that good father and grandfather. I hope I am. Maybe they will think so.

Grandpa always thought he would like to open a restaurant. If he ever had, I know it would have been a good one. When we were at their home, they always had fine china, silverware, and crystal. Teddy has the crystal with the "TCS" initials on them. Passed down from generation to generation. Keep them safe.

My grandparents did take me downtown to some nice restaurants, and one of their favorites was "Mrs. Hullings Cafeteria". Pop never had his restaurant and I wonder what other dreams and plans they may have had? He bought the farm at Gray Summit Missouri where I spent my first six years and Charles one. Pop didn't want to farm, but Dad did, and so we were farmers from 1936 to 1942.

Pop had a lot of tools, and was good at fixing things. He taught me how to use them. He believed in working hard. He often told me: "Work, work, work 'till your proud heart breaks." That never seemed like much fun, and I could only wonder if I had a "proud heart"? Was it a good thing or bad? Anyway, at 82 years of age my heart, proud or otherwise, hasn't broken yet. Besides, it's usually a girl or someone you care for who breaks your heart.

My grandpa always had a nice car. I'm sure that grandma didn't drive. Most women didn't drive back then. My own mother never drove. He always had a nice car which he referred to as his "machine". I think most of them were 4 door Dodges, but I don't remember. They always put me in the back seat.

One day while going through Forest Park on the way to the Zoo, my door flew open and out I went. Fortunately I wasn't run over nor hurt too bad. Pop suspected that I had been fooling with the door handle, but I swore I wasn't. Never would. Honest Injun! I'm not sure he was convinced but we were all glad I wasn't hurt bad. You can learn more of life with Pop and grandma from Chapter Three: Farm Life, in the "Accidental Lawyer".

Life changed when they decided to leave Webster and move to St. Petersburg, Florida around 1952.

In 1955 at Christmas time Dad, Charles, Dad's wife Donna and I drove to St. Pete to spend Christmas with them. It was a great trip because dad let me do most of the driving. However, Sharon and I were hot and heavy then, and I hated being away from her and Webster at Christmas. Christmas in Florida is pretty weird too. Sure you could hear old Bing Crosby sing White Christmas in all the stores but I guarantee you there is no snow in St. Petersburg. It was great spending time with them and that was the last time we saw grandpa alive. He died of a heart attack, and grandma moved back to Webster.

Grandpa doesn't have a grave to visit because he wasn't buried. Following his wishes he was cremated, and dad rented a plane to spread his ashes over St. Pete Bay. We got to see grandma until she died in 1965.

Grandma lived with Aunt Helen in Webster and with dad in Aledo, Illinois. She died in Webster and no grave either. My heart was broken when she was sick and passed. I was in law school at St. Louis University. I bawled like a baby and begged her not to go. Instead of me consoling her, she was consoling me. She said that was a promise she couldn't keep but she would try her best to hang around. I guess that's all any of us can do. I know I'm trying hard not to go. Grandpa was born on the 3rd day of April 1881 and died on the 26th day of March 1956 in St. Petersburg, Florida. Grandma was born the 25th day of February 1885 and died on the 3rd day of February 1965 in St. Louis, Missouri.

So far so good!

Ted & Mae B. Salveter
Nebraska 1938

Ted & Mae B. Salveter
St. Petersburg 1952

Ted Salveter Sr.

Mae B. Salveter
St. Pet, Florida 1952

Ted Salveter Sr.
St. Louis MO 1944

Old Oak Manor Hotel
LaMay MO 1948

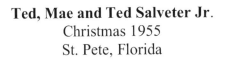

Ted, Mae and Ted Salveter Jr.
Christmas 1955
St. Pete, Florida

CHAPTER FOUR

GRANDPA AND GRANDMA OBERHAUS

I never lived with grandpa and grandma Oberhaus like I did with grandpa and grandma Salveter on the farm at Gray Summit. But we got to spend time with them because the farm was only about ten miles from Washington. At that time they owned a building on Hooker and 5th street. Grandpa's shoe shop took up half of the downstairs, and a small grocery store the other half. The second floor was where they lived, and where we stayed when we visited. Grandpa O used to take me down the street to the Blue Goose Cafe. I don't know what he had but I always had a big orange soda.

After that they lived in other houses around Washington. Grandpa must have retired and sold his building. The last house I remember was a red brick bungalow somewhere near the city park and swimming pool. This is the house grandma died in, and maybe where grandpa died too. I took swimming lessons in the park pool. They always had a big annual picnic and fish fry at the park and I remember those fondly. The park wasn't too far from the Missouri River.

Grandpa O was a generous man and lots of people borrowed money from him that they didn't repay. He wasn't flashy and was pretty stooped over. Probably from repairing those shoes. He liked his cigars and he and grandma played some serious card games. One of their favorite places to eat was Lottman's, and you could get a fantastic roast beef sandwich there.

Unlike my grandparents Salveter I don't remember Henry and Christine being particularly religious. I don't remember ever going to church with them, but I know my mom Nelda was raised in the E & R church.

A great story about them was that Christine, who was raised Catholic, got a lot of flak from the local priest for considering marriage to Henry who was not Catholic. He gave them both grief about it even after they were married. He urged Henry to convert. One Sunday the priest visited their home in Washington and Henry was sitting on the front porch. The priest insisted that Henry become Catholic. Finally grandpa snapped. He grabbed an ax that was on the front porch and proceeded to chase the poor priest down the road, wielding his trusty ax. Fortunately no one was injured and that ended the religious discussions.

When Grandma O died we were living in Webster. We were all in the kitchen and Mom answered the phone in the living room. She was nearly hysterical when she ran into the kitchen and told us Grandma had died of a massive heart attack. I was about twelve and Charles seven. Her funeral was in Washington, but we kids were not allowed. It was hard for me to believe that this strong German woman could die. It was my first encounter with death, but unfortunately not the last.

All grandparents were now deceased except Grandma Salveter. She died in 1965, and got to see me become a lawyer. Grandpa Henry was born July 5th, 1882 and died on November 3rd 1957. Grandma Christine was born September 18th, 1891 and died November 17th, 1947. There were 11 kids in Henry's family. Walter, Julius, Armond, Freddy, Clara, Elnora, Hilda, Ida and William. They all lived at 507 Hooker Street which was owned by Grandma Anna Feldmueller Oberhaus. Most never married.

Henry Oberhaus
1937

Christine Oberhaus
1937

Henry & Christine Oberhaus
Shoe Shop 1937

**Bud, Grandma and
Raymond Oberhaus,
Skip & Charles
Salveter**
Washington MO 1942

**Henry Oberhaus,
Skip &Charles
Salveter**
Christmas 1942

16

CHAPTER FIVE

OBERHAUS UNCLES

My mom had three brothers. They were good uncles to me and Charles. Melvin "Bud" Oberhaus was the baby and the last to die. They were all born in Washington, Missouri. Uncle Bud was born on the 8TH day of September, 1919, and died on the 27th day of September, 2000. They are all buried in the St. Peter's Cemetery.

Uncle Bud was married to Aunt Verna Sussmann, born January 28, 1918 and died May 25, 2012. They had two children M.J. Oberhaus, and Becky Lee Oberhaus Gable. Most of their life they lived in Union, Missouri at 1112 W. State. MJ was born August 11, 1950 and has four children. He graduated from S.E. Missouri State with a music major. He has taught music most of his life. Becky was born September 1st,1952 and graduated from Union High School. She is married to Joe Gable and has no children.

Although I loved all my uncles, Uncle Bud was my favorite and the one I had the most contact with. Not only in Union. They would come into Webster a lot. When he would come see us he would always stop by White Castle and pick up a bag of their greasy hamburgers. They are still in business. Who knows how many heart attacks they have caused? We loved 'em before we knew how bad they were for us.

I spent the whole summer with Uncle Bud and Aunt Verna before my 7th or 8th grade. Uncle Bud owned the Western Auto Stores in Union and Gerald. I worked for room and board and a little spending money. I also got to know a few of the local girls pretty well. Like Iola Allen and Dixie Stites. Uncle Bud was more supportive than Aunt Verna. I also got pretty close with my young cousins M.J. and Becky. Before I started law school and got married in 1957 I lived with them again and worked for Lee Young, an attorney and CPA in Washington and Union. No girls that summer, I was twenty-one and engaged.

When I started Drury in 1954. Uncle Bud came to Webster, loaded up his Buick with my stuff, Mom, me, and Charles. He brought us safely to Springfield and Fairbanks Hall. Where was Dad? Uncle Bud looked after his big sis and her boys.

Uncle Bud always had nice cars, and a boat or a house boat. Eventually, he also had a cabin on the Gasconade River near Herman. He was a lot of fun and introduced Charles and I to Stag Beer. Wouldn't drink anything else. After I became an attorney I had the opportunity to return some of those favors. He had a free lawyer for the rest of his life. I may have been the only lawyer he didn't think was crooked. He was proud that I became one, but he always referred to my "license to steal".

I also had the opportunity to live with my uncle Raymond Oberhaus. He was married to my Aunt Venetta Carr. When uncle Raymond was a boy, he was riding his bicycle on the foundation of a house being built. Unfortunately, he fell off and broke his hip. The surgeries were poorly done and he walked with a limp and in pain the rest of his life. He and Aunt Venetta had no children. When we moved from Mayfield, Kentucky back to St. Louis, we lived in a two-story flat on Big Bend near Clayton Road in Richmond Heights. I was in 3rd grade at Bellview School. They lived with us there on the second floor. It had to be crowded. I'm sure finances were the reason a lot of people lived with relatives. When we bought the house at 548 Summit in Webster Groves they lived there too, and their bedroom was the dining room. That house had a small building out back that Uncle Raymond raised chickens in.. We would actually eat them. The back yard got pretty bloody from chickens running around without their heads. I guess we did that on the farm in Gray Summit too.

At Christmas time, Uncle Raymond got his train set out and made a display under the tree. It was fascinating. His health kept getting worse, and I remember they made a bed for him on the screened in front porch. After a while he never left the bed and I remember telling him goodbye when I left for Lockwood School. I never saw him again. He died on the porch and they took him away. Aunt Venetta moved out and later married a concrete finisher named Johnnie Barbaglia. They had one son, Mike. She was quite a lady and was in her 90's when she died at the Lake of the Ozarks living with Mike. Uncle Raymond was born November 11, 1911 and died July 22, 1946

Uncle Raymond fought the good fight.

Uncle Lester was a very quiet loving man. He and Aunt Edna had two children, Lester Oberhaus, Jr."Junie" and Jean Oberhaus. They lived in Washington mostly and for a while in Gray Summit and Villa Ridge when Uncle Lester worked for Ollie Tatz, building quonset huts. Uncle Lester was a hard working guy, but never set the world on fire. Not many did in those days. He was born April 18, 1909. He died on the 5th day of November, 1988. Aunt Edna died years later in Chesterfield, Missouri while living near or with Jean. She was born September 13, 1908.

Uncle Lester was without a doubt my strongest uncle. He was lean, and had a chiseled body. I doubt that anybody messed with him. "The Quiet Man" for sure.

Junie was born June 7th 1929 and died in or near Washington D.C. He was quite successful I believe. Jean lives in Manchester, Missouri and is a widow. She had two sons. James Froning born in 1961 and Jeffery Froning born in 1963. Jean was married to Harold Wiley until his death on March 26, 2016. He was born November 27, 1923. Jean was born February 14,1939.

Cousins – Ted Salveter III, Jean Oberhaus Wiley, Charles Salveter, Becky Oberhaus Gable, M.J. Oberhaus
January 26, 2008

**Aunt Verna,
Ted Salveter &
Uncle Bud
Gasconade River**
July 13, 1998

**Uncle Bud,
Skip Salveter &
Aunt Verna**
July, 4, 2015

**Uncle Raymond Oberhaus & Aunt
Vanetta Oberhaus Barbaglia
1945**

**Aunt Edna and Uncle Lester
Oberhaus, Nelda O. Salveter,
Uncle Bud and Aunt Verna
Oberhaus
1981**

**Uncle Lester & Aunt Edna Oberhaus, Ted Salveter,
Aunt Verna & Uncle Bud Oberhaus**
October 10, 1980

CHAPTER SIX

NELDA MARIE ANNA OBERHAUS SALVETER

M y mother was a special lady. I guess most sons feel that way about their Moms, but I was lucky when I got her.

She had a long name. Nelda Marie Anna Oberhaus Salveter. Her family shortened that to "Girlie" and to me and Charles she was just "Mom". She was born on October 10, 1915 in Washington, Missouri and died on June 30, 1983 of colon cancer in my home at 1635 E. Delmar, Springfield, Missouri. She was only sixty-seven.

I don't know what a saint looks like but I'm pretty sure she would look like Mom. She was raised in the E & R church and was a Christian Scientist (dad's religion) most of her life. There are no official saints in either church.

Charles and I were raised Christian Scientists, but neither of us remained affiliated when we became adults. Somehow we got through that part of our lives without the aid of doctors or medicine. Mom and Dad did too, but in the end C.S. was no match for the cancer, and neither were the doctors. When Mom knew she was dying and her faith in God had not saved her, she gave me her King James Bible, and told me that she had devoted her life to it, and she no longer believed. Her horrible sickness and death was one of the things that began much doubt in my own mind. She deserved much better than she got.

Mom was a good athlete. Too bad she was born before there were many sports opportunities for girls. She did play basketball and ran track for Washington high school. She was such a fast runner that she was dubbed "The fastest girl in Franklin County". She understood the double meaning of that. Maybe being fast was what got Dad's attention. He was six years older and a Webster Groves city boy prowling around Washington. She and Dad were married in Washington on the Fourth day of August, 1934, and divorced on the eighteenth day of April, 1952 in St. Louis county. It was Dad's idea and his fault.

Back then divorce was not as common as it is now. I was pretty young when it happened and I remember an older relative took me by the shoulders, looked me in the eye and said, "Well, Skipper, you are now the man of the house.". I think I was quite shocked by that and wasn't sure I was up to the job. The way it worked was I thought I got to boss my little brother around. I did that pretty often. But Mom was the boss and the three of us made a pretty good life for ourselves.

Dad paid a small amount of child support, but it wasn't enough and Mom had to find work. It seemed we were always financially challenged but she did a great job of raising us and providing for us. I felt insecure for a long time because of that divorce, and I vowed that if I ever married and had kids of my own I would never put them through that. She kept the house and it became our rock, our sense of stability. I think that whole experience is why Charles and I think about 548 and Webster the way we do. It was our safe place in our upside down world.

I'm not sure what the first job Mom had was after the divorce, but I believe it was in the ladies department at Lammerts Department Store on Lockwood Avenue in Webster. An old gentleman named Mr. Lowry owned it. Mom had many happy years there. When dad left we had no car and Mom didn't drive. Lots of people gave us rides to church and various places, but mostly we rode the streetcar and later the bus. That's how Mom got to work. I remember one morning we woke up to heavy snow and ice, and I saw Mom struggling to get up the hill on Greely Avenue to catch the streetcar. She was on her hands and knees, crawling up and sliding back. Most employees probably just stayed home. Not her. She was one in a million.

After Lammerts she managed Bascomb's Ladies Wear in the Yorkshire Shopping Center in Webster. Kurt Bascomb was in

Charles' class of 1959 at Webster High. Webster Groves had a train station on Gore Avenue. Passenger trains were used less and less and the railroad closed the station and put it up for sale. A guy named Harvey Kassabaum bought it and made a ladies shop out of it called The Station Store. Mom managed that until 1982 when the cancer appeared.

It was unbelievable to me how many people who shopped in each place she worked loved her and thought so highly of her. She made her family proud.

The reason people felt this way was because she gave out unconditional love and touched so many lives. Her education ended at high school, but she was a person of great wisdom and strength. Even so, she didn't always say what she meant.

Once when we were celebrating the Fourth of July at Charles' home in Springfield we were all enjoying the beautiful evening and watching her grandchildren shoot off their fireworks. She gave a big sigh and said: "Oh, I'm so delightful."

She handled the kidding well, and always humored the kids who wanted her to take out her false teeth and show them. Occasionally, she was also a little confused about theology and religion.

One time in 1967 when I was standing with her in Wisconsin viewing a geological wonder that was over a million years old, she said, "Was that before the time of Christ?"

I assured her it was. Another time I suggested to her that she might want to scrap her King James Bible and get a better translation. She adamantly refused and said: "If it was good enough for Jesus it's good enough for me."

I didn't have the heart to tell her Jesus had no bible, and the King James was written around 1611 in England. Many "Christians" are confused by such things.

I mentioned that she was a fast runner in high school. She was, but I didn't believe she still was. I never ever saw her run and people didn't jog in those days. I was probably about fourteen and full of it. She got off the bus and I greeted her in front of the house. I don't know which of us suggested a footrace but we had one to the next corner. I was sure I would smoke her. There she was in a dress and ladies shoes and me in jeans and tennis shoes. She took off like a shot and easily beat me. We never raced again and I never spoke of it. She was surely the fastest Mom in Webster Groves.

When our family and Charles' visited her in that small house, she always had a bed for the ten of us. She'd let the kids eat breakfast in the living room and watch TV while we slept in. No matter how much I hoped she wouldn't pull out the sugary cereals, she always did and spoiled them rotten. It's what grandmas do.

For some strange reason I always thought I would retire back in Webster and live with Mom. Maybe I'd teach classes at Webster University, and follow all the Statesmen sports. I could see myself reading and drinking coffee at the Library on Saturday mornings.

That probably would never have worked out, and it all ended when she got sick in 1982 and died in 1983. Right or wrong, Charles and I sold the house and all the plans and dreams with it.

Life doesn't always work out the way you hoped.

Ted, Nell & Charles Salveter
1953

**Charles, Nell
& Ted Salveter
1957**

Nell Oberhaus Salveter
Confirmation 1927

Nell Oberhaus Salveter
Washington High School
Graduation 1933

CHAPTER SEVEN

THEODORE C. SALVETER JR. (DAD)

P art scoundrel, part sage. Wise and foolish too. No matter what you thought of my dad he was at times a larger than life character. As far as I know he never wrote anything about himself. Not many do. He wasn't an enormous success in life, not by most standards, but if we knew all about it, it might knock your socks off.

He's long gone, and so are so many others who could shed light on this piece.

Dad was born on April 11, 1909 in Lincoln, Nebraska to Theodore Clifton Salveter and Mae B. Salveter. His only sibling was his older sister Helen Salveter Wardan. Other Salveters in our line lived in the St. Louis area in St. Charles and Webster Groves. Of all those places, Webster was the most important in his life and certainly in mine. Dad's life ended in Springfield, Missouri at Manor Care on July 9, 1995 at age eighty-six.

He had been up and down, but rallied and stabilized a lot. Charles and I thought I could leave on a family vacation to Oregon and Washington. We had only been there a day or so when Charles called me to tell me Dad had passed that morning. I guess he couldn't wait for me to come home. Apparently he knew it was his time because he told his nurse that morning he wouldn't be needing his meds anymore.

Now he was gone, and all the questions I meant to ask and should have asked could not be asked. How foolish we are to procrastinate and think there will always be time. Thankfully brother Charles had been talking with Dad about these things. Just one more thing for me to regret.

Dad started his life in Nebraska because grandpa Salveter who grew up in St. Charles, Missouri drifted up there and met grandma who grew up in the Council Bluffs, Iowa area. Her maiden name was Snider, and her family was in the grocery business. She probably attended Rockford College, Illinois around 1903. My grandparents got together and were married in Nebraska.

Grandpa Salveter was a salesman for M.E. Smith Company in Lincoln, Omaha, and York. Both Dad and Aunt Helen started school in Nebraska, maybe at the York College Demonstration School. They bought some property in Canada in 1912 and lived there only a short while because grandma didn't like it much. From there they moved to Webster Groves on Sunnyside Avenue. Dad claimed he had gone to grade school in Lincoln with General John Pershing's son.

In Webster, dad and Aunt Helen went to Lockwood grade school, Webster Junior High and Webster High School. The same schools Charles and I went to. Dad graduated in 1929 and was an outstanding athlete in football and baseball. He went on to Missouri University to play football. He was a member of Kappa Alpha, and probably paid more attention to the temptations of Fraternity and college life, and not enough of studies and football. I'm sure that he regretted that. So he never finished college, and who knows how good his football career might have been.

Three brother's Henry, Charles, and Louis Salveter built three homes on Plant Avenue in Webster which can be seen on the Historic Walk.

The family had been successful in dry goods business and one of the locations of Stewart and Salveter was on Grand Avenue in St. Louis near the famous Fox Theatre. This is why grandpa was in that line also, for Bradley and Famous Barr.

Dad was a good salesman with a great gift of gab. He never met a stranger, and rarely ever told the same joke twice. Sometime after his aborted college experience he had different jobs, and somehow met Mom on a blind date I think in Washington, Missouri.

Mom and Dad were married in Washington in 1934, and moved

to the farm grandpa owned at Gray Summit. Dad wanted to be a farmer. Grandpa wasn't.

I was born in 1936 and Charles in 1941.

The farm thing didn't work out for dad and we moved to Mayfield, Kentucky in 1942 so dad could work for Ralston Purina. After a couple of years we moved to Richmond Heights. Dad worked for McDonald Douglas as an inspector for airplanes. He worked various places such as Goldies' Department Store and Western Auto.

We lived with Aunt Helen in Webster for a short while and then on November 10, 1944 bought the house at 548 Summit in Webster from Patrick and Genevieve Monohan. That was to be "home" until Mom died in 1983.

Dad left us in 1951 and divorced Mom in 1952 in St. Louis County. He remarried Donna Robotham who had one son Richard Robotham. Dad and Donna had Celia Marie Salveter born April 11, 1954 in St. Louis. She died in Arlington, Texas. She never married and had no children. They also had Robert Salveter who was born on August 9, 1956 in Aledo, Illinois. He is married to Jeri, retired from the Air Force, and lives in Las Vegas, Nevada. He also had no children.

In 1955 or so Dad was transferred by Western Auto to Davenport, Iowa. He got to know "old Sam" who owned the Western Auto Store in Aledo, Illinois. Dad quit his job and bought the store. He operated that until 1966 when he sold it and moved to Greenwood Avenue in Springfield, Missouri to be near Charles and me.

Bob and Celia went to Eugene Field Elementary, Pershing Junior High and Glendale High School. Celia graduated from Glendale and Bob from Ozark High School.

Dad moved to Christian County and built an "in the ground home" on thirty acres near Linden, Missouri. It was his dream or plan for all of us to build houses there and have a "Salveter Compound" like the Kennedys I suppose. No one wanted to do it, and I wasn't about to drive to the Greene County Courthouse or my office every day. Eventually Dad and Donna divorced, the property was sold, and the dream forgotten.

Bob made a good career out of the Air Force and Celia made her own way until her death in Texas.

Although dad retired when he sold the store, he was really too young to do it, and held a multitude of jobs in Springfield. Some of them I got for him. He was a clerk in the Magistrate Court of Judge Ed Barbour, an auditor for Haskill Holman, the Missouri State Auditor, an insurance salesman and others. He even worked in my law firm for a time.

Eventually he moved from the Ozark Park a Home trailer park to Brownsville, Texas, and lived there for several years until Charles and I brought him home. His Parkinson's was getting bad and he needed help. In 1991 we moved him into the Montclair Retirement Home until he went to Manor Care where he passed away in 1995.

When that happened about everything he owned could be and was put in a medium sized cardboard box. What a strange end for such a long life.

One thing he did leave behind were some of his favorite sayings. If you had a job or task to do, but weren't getting it done, he might say, "Do something even if it's wrong!"

If he thought you were going to make a bad mistake, he might say. "Don't be a stumph." Or if you had a problem with someone his advice might be, "Tell them what Ole the Swede would tell them--Go kissa da ass!" And if you were so sure about someone or something, he might caution with "Vas you there, Charlie?"

He had a million of them!

Dad is buried in Maple Park Cemetery along with my son Philip Anthony Salveter and wife Sharon Lee Downen Salveter.

There's room for more.

Rest in peace.

Bob and Celia Salveter
1960

Celia & Bob Salveter, Tony & Teddy Salveter
Christmas 1964

Chief Master Sergeant Robert D. Salveter

CMSgt Robert D Salveter was born 9 August 1956 in Aledo Illinois. He attended High School in Ozark Missouri, where he was active in sports and most everything else but academics.

Chief Salveter entered the Air Force in June 1974. After completing Basic Training he received his technical training as a Missile Systems Analyst

Specialist at Chanute AFB, Illinois.

Upon Technical School graduation, Chief Salveter's first assignment was to the Electro-Mechanical Team Section, 91st Organizational Missile Maintenance Squadron, 91st Strategic Missile Wing, Minot AFB, North Dakota.

While at Minot, he quickly progressed from an Electro-Mechanical Technician, to a Team Chief. After reenlisting he applied for a base of preference assignment.

In September 1978 he was reassigned to the 394th ICBM Test Maintenance Squadron Vandenberg AFB, California where he got his first experience with the follow-on Operational Test and Evaluation business.

For the next 6 years he performed as an Electro-Mechanical Team Chief, Instructor and Evaluator. During this period he performed as an Electro-Mechanical Team Chief, Instructor and Evaluator. During this period he became qualified on all three Minuteman weapons systems and was involved in over 40 test launches and two major weapon systems modifications.

In October 1984, Chief Salveter was selected for reassignment to the 391st Strategic Missile Evaluation Squadron as a Strategic Air Command Electro-Mechanical Team Evaluator. Here he performed 22 evaluations at the 6 missile wings, was involved with the development of the Peacekeeper weapon system and was one of the EMT evaluators for the 1988 OLYMPIC Arena Exercise.

After a 4 year stint in the SMES he then went to the Air Force Operational Test and Evaluation Center where he worked on the last initial Operational Test and Evaluation Peacekeeper launch and the early phases of Peacekeeper Rail Garrison program. In early 1989 the Strategic Air Command said we need Salveter back at Minot AFB, so in September he was reassigned to the 91st Field Missile Maintenance Squadron as Superintendent of the EMT Branch, the very same shop where he was a first term airman.

In January 1991, he was selected as NCOIC of Job Control and soon thereafter as Superintendent of the Job Control Flight, 91st Maintenance Support Squadron. In June 1993, he was sent to the 91st Field Missile Maintenance Squadron as Superintendent of Facility Maintenance Flight.

While at Minot he helped the wing maintain the highest Missile Alert Rate in the command for five consecutive years. In July of 1994, Chief Salveter returned to Vandenberg as Maintenance superintendent of the 2nd Space Launch Squadron where he was fortunate enough to be involved with the last three launches of the Atlas E. Rocket in the Air Force inventory.

Soon after being selected for Chief in late 1995 a Senior Airman form the Air Force Personnel center Chief's group called and told the Chief he was being reassigned to the 576th Flight Test Squadron and in February 1996 he became Superintendent of the Quality Assurance Flight.

In November 1997 he moved to the Superintendent of the Generation Flight. In March 1999, she was assigned to his present position as the 576th Flight Test Squadron Maintenance Superintendent. In this position, the Chief served as the Senior Enlisted Maintenance Manager responsible for the production efforts of 325 highly specialized technicians and supervisors in support of AFSPC's $350

Million Minuteman and Peacekeeper Force Development Evaluation Program.

CMSgt Salveter has been recognized for many extraordinary achievements throughout his distinguished career. In June 1982, he was selected as the 394th Test Maintenance Squadron Maintenance Airman of the Month. He was Minot Air Force Base's SNCO of the Quarter in 1995. He was a distinguished Graduate of NCO Leadership School in 1980. He won the Academic Achievement Award and was a Distinguished Graduate at the NCO Academy in 1987 and was a Distinguished Graduate from the Air Force Senior NCO Academy in 1991. He earned his CCAF degree in 1989 and a Bachelors of Science Degree in 1994.

Chief Salver wears the ICBM Master Technician, Team Chief, Instructor and Evaluator Badges. His awards and decorations include the Meritorious Service Medal with one oak leaf clusters, the Air Force Commendation Medal, the Air Force Achievement Medal, with three oak leaf clusters, the Air Force Outstanding Unit Award, the Air Force Good Conduct Medal, the National Defense Service Medal with one oak leaf cluster, the Air Force Longevity Service Award, the NCO Professional Military Education Graduate Ribbon with two oak leaf clusters and the Air Force Training Ribbon.

Chief Salveter is Married to the former Jerilyn K Dial of Springfield, Illinois.

Bob & Jeri Salveter

AQUARIUS: "CRAZY 4 POKER"

The **Aquarius** is one of the few Laughlin casinos to hold tournaments in table games such as **Let It Ride**, **Crazy 4 Poker** and **Three Card Poker**. They recently held one such tournament for Crazy 4 Poker fans that resulted in two ties—a tie for the first place prize and a tie for third place. The Aquarius wound up pooling the prize money for first and second and split it 50/50, doing the same with the prize money marked for third and fourth places. The winners were (*pictured above, l to r*): **Charles Lewis**, Grants Pass, Oregon tied for 1st and won **$8,500**; **Donald Cross** of Goodyear, Arizona, **$3,500** for 5th place; **Robert Salveter** of Laughlin, tied for 3rd place, **$4,250**; **Jeffrey Zeesman** of Encino, California, **$2,500** for 6th; **Paz Hernandez** (seated) of Los Angeles, tied for 3rd, **$4,250**; **Daniel Wehler** of Redwood Falls, Minnesota, tied for 1st, **$8,500**. The next table game tournament at the Aquarius is a **Let It Ride tourney** on December 8-9; see this page

12-13-12

**Ted & Donna
Salveter
Bobby & Celia**
August 1961

St. Louis Daily Globe-Democrat, Thursday Morning, November 7, 1929.

hmen Over Whelm Washington U

Webster Groves Youths Starring on Tiger Frosh

Carl Yeckel, left, and Ted Salveter, two Webster Groves youths, members of the University of Missouri freshman football squad, have been named by Coach Anton J. Stankowski in his tentative starting lineup for the game between the Tiger freshmen and the University of Nebraska first-year eleven at Lincoln next Saturday. Salveter is a tackle, and Carl Yeckel center.

Ted and Nell Salveter

CHAPTER EIGHT

AUNT HELEN GARDNER SALVETER WARDAN

My Aunt and dad's only sibling was Helen Gardner Salveter Warden born on the 14th day of May, 1906 and died on the 3rd day of May, 1979 in Summerville, South Carolina. She had two children, Patricia Helen Wardan and Charles Randal Wardan. She lost several by miscarriage. She was buried in Bel Fountain Neighbors in St. Louis, MO. She was living with Pat when she died.

Like my dad, she grew up in Nebraska and Webster Groves, Missouri. She was a few years older than dad and also went to Lockwood Grade School, Webster Junior High and Webster High School. She attended Stephen's College in Columbia, and may have graduated from there. She married Charles Wardan who predeceased her.

Most of the time they lived at 327 Greeley Avenue in Webster. It was an English Tudor mansion. Randy and Pat went to Avery Grade School, Webster Junior High and Webster High, but the family moved to Kirkwood and they graduated from Kirkwood High.

I don't know all she did, but when she was young and fresh out of college, she was Augustus Busch's personal secretary. He gave her a fancy cigarette case, (she didn't smoke) and we still have it. Anheuser-Busch has done quite well since then.

At a much later time, 1953-1973, she was the secretary to the Dean of Eden Theological Seminary in Webster.

She was a loving aunt. On many Thanksgiving and Christmas holidays we would have great dinners with them. Uncle Charlie would always flock the tree and decorate it completely.

I'm not sure that Dad and Aunt Helen got along all that well, especially after he left Mom. He wasn't at those later meals. Aunt Helen was very fond of murder mysteries and read the Bible a lot. Go figure. She also loved playing canasta.

Randy had an elaborate train set up, and Pat always walked on her toes. Wanted to look taller I guess. Randy loved to fish and do woodworking.

Randy was married in 1968 and divorced Janice Wardan in 2002. They lived in Eugene, Oregon with their two boys, Robert and Scott Warden. Randy was ten years younger than me. He was born January 13, 1946 in St. Louis and died in Eugene Oregon on April 23, 2004. His ashes are in Lake LBJ, Marble Falls, Texas.

Randy graduated from Kirkwood High School in 1964, and Drake University in 1968. He was a systems analyst for McDonald Douglas. He also owned his own software company in Eugene, Oregon.

Pat had four girls and lives in Georgetown, Texas. She married William James McMillan on June 26, 1999.

Uncle CHARLES MONROE WARDAN was born August 21, 1900 in St. Louis and died October 20, 1962. He also is buried in Bel Fountain Neighbors. He was a salesman for the Bradley line and clothing companies. He was a good uncle. He had an attractive mustache and if he hadn't been bald may have looked like Clark Gable. Who knows?

He was an officer in the CCC, and among other things directed and commanded the park and trout farm project at Roaring River in Cassville, Missouri. Dad always said Uncle Charlie got into some kind of trouble there and to never mention I was related if in that area. What could it have been?

Uncle Charlie had five brothers and sisters. In 1917 he lied about his age and joined the Army to fight in World War I. He was injured in battle in France. He rose to the rank of Captain. His father had a clothing manufacturing company where he worked until the company went bankrupt.

Because of the great depression he attended Washington

University but did not graduate. He was quite the gardener and loved fishing and carpentry. That's where Randy got it. I remember he took me fishing to southern Missouri when I was quite young. We stopped in Crocker, Missouri to meet a relative. Dru Salveter who with his wife Mae, Owned the Bank of Crocker and several businesses. I became good friends with them after I started practicing law until they both died.

Grandma Mae Salveter lived for a while with dad in Aledo, Illinois where he owned the Western Auto Store. After Uncle Charles died she moved to Webster and lived with Aunt Helen until her death.

Aunt Helen spent time with mom, and I know they went to the Christian Science Church in Webster across from the High school at 100 Selma Avenue. That was mine and Charles' church too until I got married to Sharon Downen in the Webster Baptist Church on Summit Avenue in 1957.

I don't remember her death. I was practicing law in Springfield, Missouri and raising a family. It's like both Aunt Helen and Uncle Charlie just disappeared from my life, just slipped away with no fanfare, no drama.

One other thing that I remember was I mowed their big yard with a push mower. What a task for a kid!

I also remember their big dog Colonel took a big chunk out of my leg when I rode my bike into their yard.

The good old days!

Pat was born June 9th 1944 in St. Louis, MO. She graduated from Kirkwood High School in 1962. She has an A D N from Meramec College, 1972 and a BSN from St. Louis University in 1976, and a MSN from Med University of South Carolina in 1989. She worked in nursing for 34 years and retired in 2006. She was a staff nurse, Nursing instructor, Nurse Manager and Chief Nursing Officer.

Pats four children are Deborah Beagle of Thornton, Colorado, Kelly Wendt of Anderson, South Carolina, Tracey Klinger of Summerville, South Carolina and Laura Medrano of Round Rock, Texas

Aunt Helen and Pat Wardan
1945

Helen and Randy
Wardan Teddy Salveter
Christmas 1960

Best wishes for a

Merry Christmas

Charles, Helen,
Pat & Randy — Wardan

Helen Wardan, Teddy Salveter, Charles Wardan, Nell Salveter, Sharon Salveter, Charles Salveter & Mae B Salveter
Christmas 1960 548 Summit

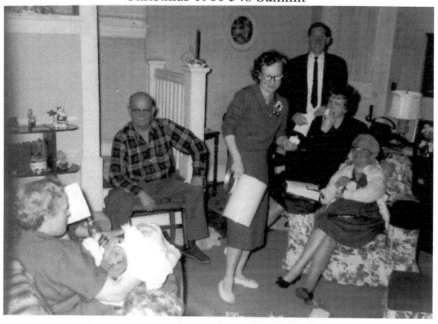

327 Greeley

**Charles Warden, Sharon Downan, Ted Salveter,
Helen Wardan, Dick Miller & Nell Salveter**
1956, 548 Summit

**Helen & Charles Wardan, Sharon Salveter, Nell Salveter,
Randy Wardan, Teddy Salveter & Mae B. Salveter**
Christmas 1960

Helen, Teddy, Ted, Nell & Mae B. Salveter
1960

Charles & Skip Salveter & Pat Wardan
Old Oak Manor Hotel - 1946

CHAPTER NINE

CHARLES ROBERT SALVETER

My little brother Charlie was born on February 16, 1941 in St. Frances Hospital, in Washington, Missouri. I was almost 5 when he showed up. Old Doc Mays, the same one who pulled me into this world, hauled brother out too. He did a good job because 1 couldn't ask for a better brother.

Sure, we've had our moments these past seventy-seven or so years, but as we grew older he has been like a rock, helping me through my life, the good and the bad.

We still lived on the farm at Gray Summit in 1941, but moved a year or so later to Mayfield, Kentucky. The person who knows the most about his life is Charlie himself. Hopefully, he'll tell it. I'll tell what I know or remember.

When Charles was born they took me to the hospital to meet him. I'm not sure I was too thrilled that this competition had arrived. Somebody thought it was a good idea for me to give him a birthday gift. A welcome to my world present. I think it was a toy truck or something. Well, I don't think I wanted to give it up, but they "didn't give me no choice." Thus started the program of little brother getting the good stuff. It went on until mom passed away in 1983.

I was forty-seven and he was forty-two. My hand-me-downs weren't good enough for him. I got cheap shirts and he got McGregors. I learned not too long ago that while mom sent me a much appreciated one dollar a week when I was at Drury College, she sent Five dollars to him. It's too horrible to go on. Of course he doesn't remember it all quite the way I do.

I started the first grade in Mayfield. The school had some kind of contest to pick the best or cutest baby, and baby brother won! I didn't win any blue ribbons. Our time in Mayfield was only a couple of years, but one day when we were outside playing on the sidewalk, he got excited and said, "Look, a spider on the corn crink!"

Well, it was funny at the time.

We left Mayfield so dad could take a job in St. Louis building airplanes for the War. We moved into a crummy upstairs flat at Big Bend and Clayton Road. Little Rusty Lewis lived in the downstairs.

One day little Rusty split brother's head with a hatchet. All his life he has been hard headed. Good thing. He's had a few blows to it.

We finally moved to 548 Summit in Webster Groves.

When he started kindergarten at Lockwood Grade School in 1946 I was in the 5th grade. For two years I watched out for him like a big brother should. After that we were never in the same school again, and he was on his own. When he was in kindergarten I remember watching him through the closed door. Those kids used a lot of gray clay, and he loved to eat his.

When dad left us in 1951 or so I remember that some adult told me I was now the head of the house. I took that to mean I should boss him around. One day he refused to do what I commanded and so I got his arm behind his back and kept twisting until he agreed to obey. He was so hard-headed he didn't care even if I broke his arm. Finally, I was afraid I would break his arm so I gave up. The kid was tough. Or stupid. Or maybe both.

Since we were poor we made a lot of our own toys. I made a bow and some arrows that weren't too straight. Charles was riding his bike or trike out front on the sidewalk. For whatever reason I demanded that he stop or I would shoot. He didn't stop. I shot at his tires. That crooked arrow started at the tire but curved up and hit him in the eye.

Mom wasn't home. I was scared. He was scared and bleeding. I caught holy hell when she got home. I came close to putting his eye out. A horrible thought that upsets me even today.

You might think that I always gave the kid a bad time. Not so. Well, there was the time I shot my BB gun at a fish or snake in a creek and the BB ricocheted off a rock and hit him in the face. I didn't mean to.

No, most of our life together was good. Except for the times I would crawl under his bed at night and make noises like the flying monkeys in the Wizard of Oz.

Boy, did that freak him out.

There are many wonderful memories.

One year near Christmas, we waited for mom to get home from work to give us some money to buy a Christmas tree. It was dark, and after dinner we pulled our sled through the snow and cold to Old Orchard Gardens. We picked out a nice one, put it on the sled and headed for home to show mom. We got all the decorations out and put up the best tree we ever had. What a great memory.

One summer we were swimming at Waterloo County Club in Illinois. There was a big slide and diving boards out in the middle. A roped off shallow swimming area was at the beach. Charles was supposed to stay there where it was safe while I was out on the diving boards. I guess he decided he was going to try to swim out where all the big guys were. I saw him.

Saw him struggle and start to go under. I dove in, swam as fast as I could and found him under the water, a scary moment for all.

We made it through those times. I'm sure there are lots of stories.

Eventually I graduated from high school in 1954, and went to Drury College. I was away most of the time except for holidays and summers at home. No telling what kind of mischief he got into.

In 1957 I got married to Sharon and started law school at St. Louis University. I wasn't staying at home but I was in and around Webster until 1960 when I graduated and moved to Springfield, Missouri.

Charles graduated from Webster in 1959 and started college at Drury. We were both Sig Eps there.

As he finished high school I got to see him wrestle and try out for football. Every Wednesday night, Sharon and I had dinner with Mom and Charles. Mom always fixed cube steaks, salad, french fries, cokes and some kind of dessert. We appreciated those free meals because our own budget for food was pretty thin.

Anyway we would watch Maverick and eat on the card table in the living room. Those were simple, but terrific times together. Life was not fancy, but very good. I got to see little brother grow up.

After law school we lived in a duplex at 2020 E. Page until we bought a house in 1961 at 1837 S. Hampton in Springfield.

Charlie transferred from Drury to SMSU, and for a while lived in one of our upstairs bedrooms. He became the favorite uncle of my two boys Teddy and Tony. They called him "Uncle Barley". At some point we started to refer to him as "the little yellow man". We had seen a show about a guy who lived in someone's attic and never went out. His skin turned yellow from never being outside. Charlie's skin didn't turn yellow.

He was a finicky eater, and dreaded it when Sharon would fix "Cherokee Casserole" for dinner. Eventually he moved into a wild apartment with some fellow students, and we never lived together again.

At some point in our childhood in Webster, I started calling him "Frongles" and he called me "Nongles". After a while we couldn't remember who was which or why we started it in the first place. We still do it today at times, especially on Christmas present tags. I have googled it, and got no answer. If you know what it means, tell us!

A lot has gone on. We both raised families, had jobs and are retired. We like to reminisce about the old days and remember those who we loved and are gone. Almost everybody is. Charles got a bachelors and masters from SMSU. He was the director for Vocational Rehabilitation in this area and did much consulting work after he retired. I love my brother, what more can I say?

Charles married Karen Pozniak December 26, 1964 and had two daughters, Amy Lynn Salveter and Lara Ann Salveter. After he and Karen divorced he has had a special friend, Shirley Vanstavern. She is like family. He lives on a four hundred acre farm near Halltown, and she in Willard. Neither Amy, or Lara, married or had children. Both graduated from Missouri State. Lara got a Masters in Social Work from KU and Amy a Masters in Ornithology from Arkansas U. Amy was born on July 8th 1968, and Lara on March 31, 1972. Both in Springfield, Missouri. Lara is in Social work, and Amy is in a successful career protecting the environment in both state and federal positions. Including the DNR and the U.S. Forest service. Both girls were good softball and basketball players for Ozark High School. Amy graduated in 1986 and Lara in 1990. Lara had a very serious basketball injury to her knee, and had to quit playing.

**Teddy, Ted,
Tony (Standing)
& Charles Salveter**
Cave at Ozark Farm
1989

**Charles & Ted Salveter
Halltown**
2016

Lara, Karen, Amy, Charles, Ted, Tony Salveter & Miriam Downen
Lara's 16th Birthday - March 1988

Teddy, Charles & Brennon Salveter
Bois D'Arc - Thanksgiving - 2009

Charles, Teddy & Ted Salveter
Farm Halltown - 2013

Charles, Teddy, Bren, Henry & Ted Salveter
Ted's 80th Birthday May 5, 2016

Charles & Skip
Charles' 65th Birthday February 16, 2006

Harold Smith, Charles Salveter, Skip Salveter & Albert Smith
1946

548 Summit, Webster Groves MO - 1945

CHAPTER TEN

THEODORE C. SALVETER III

This is the part about me. It will be short because I wrote a book that covered most of my life through 2006. It was called "The Accidental Lawyer". I also wrote a book called "His Wonderful Life", about my son Tony and one called "The Fairytale Princess" about my wife Sharon. Both Tony and Sharon predeceased me. There is much about me in those books too.

I won't try to duplicate that here in this book. I have disclosed a lot about me in writing about all those other relatives.

I was born on May 5, 1936 in St. Francis Hospital, Washington, Missouri. Old Doc Mays delivered me. My parents were Nelda Marie Anna Oberhaus Salveter and Theodore Clifton Salveter, Jr. We lived on my grandfather's farm at Gray Summit, Missouri until I was six when we moved to Mayfield, Kentucky. I started first grade at Washington Elementary and second grade at another school. We moved to St. Louis when I was in third grade at Bellview, Avery, and Lockwood.

Five grade schools in three years. Talk about being "the new kid". I learned a lot about fighting.

I finished at Lockwood and moved on for 7th and 8th grades at Webster Junior High. For my sophomore and junior years I went to Webster High and to The Principia, a prep school, for my freshman and senior years. I played football, basketball and baseball. I went to Drury on a basketball scholarship and also played tennis.

I started St. Louis University School of Law in 1957 and

graduated in 1960. Then I began to practice law in Springfield until I retired in 1997.

Sharon and I had three children, Theodore IV, Philip Anthony (Tony), and Paige Allison. Tony died March 8, 1990 and Sharon April 17, 2010.

I met and married a wonderful lady named, Becky Hogan on May 31, 2011. I was, and still am, a very lucky man.

I was in the Marine Corps reserves from 1955 to 1961. Six years. I taught Business Law and Political Science at Drury University and Missouri State University. I was elected to The Missouri Legislature in 1968 and The Springfield School Board in 1974.

I had a brother, Charles Robert, half-brother Robert, and half-sister Celia Mae (deceased)

If you want more, read the books!

Charles & Ted Salveter
1952

**Ted Jr. teaching Ted III how to block while
George Schuette looks on**
1951

**Charles, Skip &
Ted Salveter**
548 Summit
1950

Skip & Sport
Don't mess with them!
1952

Arlene, Ted, Ted III, Andy Brez & Paige Salveter
Devil's Den
October 27, 2013

**Ted III &
Ted IV**
February 16, 2016

**Ted, Sharon, Paige
Tony, Ted Salveter**
1984

Cast Announced For Trouper Play Next Semester

"The Imaginary Invalid", a comedy in three acts by Moliere, has been selected as the second play of the year to be given by the Drury Lane Troupers on March 2 and 3, according to Robert Wilhoit. This comedy by the famous French playwright was first produced by the Palais-Royale in Paris in 1673.

Those students winning parts in the play include Ralph Dickinson, Sabra Manning, Connie Elmore, Herb Branson, Jon Robb, Steve Elmore, Arthur Blume, Ted Salveter, Shilah Adams, Larry Ahlers, and Don Westerhold. There is still one part that is yet to be cast and it will be announced on Monday. Playbooks may be secured on Monday from Mr. Wilhoit.

The play deals with a man who enjoys being sick, even to the extent of trying to marry his daughter to a doctor, so that he will have continuous medication for his imaginary ills.

Moliere is world renowned for his keen and critical satires on social, professional, and moral conventions of his day and ours. It has been said that he, almost alone, among the playwrights of the seventeenth century was able to make such comedies that are applicable, regardless of age.

Drury 1955-56

60

Campaign 1970

Webster Groves Sigma Phi Epsilon Frat Brothers
Christmas
1958

Family Camp & Hike
Devil's Den, Arkansas
October 26, 2013

Last Family Thanksgiving – Touch Football game
1635 E. Delmar
1999

Skip Salveter
Current River
1967

Skip Salveter
Flag football, Drury College
1955

Ted Salveter #48
Country Day vs Principia
1953

CHAPTER ELEVEN

SHARON LEE DOWNEN SALVETER

My book, "The Fairytale Princess" is about my wife Sharon. It is pretty complete, but honestly, to write everything about anyone would take volumes.

Sharon was born on December 17, 1937 in Swedish Covenant Hospital, Chicago, Illinois. Her parents were Charles Gerald Downen and Miriam Pauline Metz Downen. She died on April 17, 2010 at Quail Creek, Springfield, Missouri. She had three siblings: Patricia Downen Biesinger, Mary Downen McConnell, and Charles Thomas Downen (deceased).

We have two grandchildren; Rachael Erin Salveter and Brennon Anthony Salveter. Three great grandchildren; Claire Salveter, Henry Anthony Salveter and Millie Salveter Rose.

Sharon was a beautiful and intelligent lady. She went to Pattonville, Missouri grade school, Webster Groves Junior High, and Webster High where she graduated in 1955. She attended Drury College 1955 - 1957, where she was a Kappa Delta. She graduated from Washington University in 1960 with a bachelor's degree in Elementary Education and later a Masters Degree from Missouri State University in Education.

She taught at Valley Park, Pattonville, and Jarrett and Hickory Hills middle schools in ESL for the Springfield Public Schools. She loved tennis, running and golf. She played the piano quite well.

She died from Alzheimer's, much too young.

Sharon Lee (Downen) Salveter

Sharon Lee (Dowen) Salveter, 72, Springfield, passed away at 8 a.m. on April 17, 2010 in Quail Creek Nursing due to complications from a fall in her home. Sharon was born on December 17, 1937 in Chicago, Illinois to Gerald and Miriam Downen. She was united in marriage to Ted C. Salveter, III on August 30, 1957 in the Webster Baptist Church, Webster Groves, Missouri.

Sharon graduated from Webster Groves highschool in 1955. She attended Drury University, and was a member of Kappa Delta Sorority. She graduated from Washington University in St. Louis in 1960 with a bachelors degree in Education, and Missouri State University with a Masters in Education in 1977. Sharon taught school in Valley Park and Pattonville in St. Louis while Ted was in law school in St. Louis University. She retired from the Springfield Public Schools in 1997 as an ESL teacher at Hickory Hills Middle School.

Sharon was a member of Avant Gard of SMMA, Twin Oaks Country Club, the YMCA, and Evangel Temple Christian Center. She taught Sunday school at University Heights Baptist Church, and Missionettes at Evangel Temple. She was an avid tennis player, ran races, did aerobics, and struggled with golf. She loved to hike and travel with her family and friends. She was a loving, caring and wonderful wife, sister and mother.

Sharon was predeceased by her parents; a son, Philip (Tony) Salveter; and a nephew Chris McConnell. She is survived by her husband Ted; children Ted Salveter, IV and his wife Arlene of Ash Grove, Paige Salveter and her husband Andy Brez of Kansas City, Missouri; sisters Pat Biesinger and husband Bob of Brownsville, Oregon, Mary McConnell and husband Anthony of Nixa; brother Tom (Chuck) Downen and his wife Sherry of Rogersville; a cousin Cristie Donohue and her husband Terry of Harrison, Arkansas; a brother in law Charles Salveter of Halltown; brother in law Bob Salveter and his wife Jeri of Laughlin, Nevada; and sister-in-law Celia Salveter of Arlington, Texas; two grandchildren, Rachael Salveter of Dallas, Texas, and Brennon Salveter of Springfield; nieces Amy and Lara Salveter, Margo McConnell Siemering and Kelly McConnell, Jeri Lynn Hawk, Sandy Biesinger, Lisa Biesinger; and nephews, Bobby Biesinger, Bob Downen, and Andy Downen. She had many dear and loving friends and fellow teachers. Our special thanks of the nurses and staff in Quail Creek Nursing and Good Shepard Hospice for the love and care they gave to her.

Services will be in Gorman-Scharpf Funeral Home on April 20, 2010 at 10 a. m. , and visitation will be in Evangel Temple Christian Church from 6 to 8 p.m. on April 19, 2010. Burial will be following in Maple Park Cemetery. In lieu of flowers memorial contributions may be made to the Tony Salveter Scholarship at William Jewell College in Liberty, Missouri, or to the charity of the donors choice.

Miss Sharon Downen Is Married at Church

MISS SHARON LEE DOWNEN and Theodore Clifton Salveter Jr. were married recently at Webster Groves Baptist Church. The Rev. Gerald Young performed the ceremony in a setting of white flowers and candlelight. Afterward the bride's parents, Mr. and Mrs. Charles Gerald Downen, gave a reception at their home, 930 Twining place, Webster Groves.

The bride wore a white silk gown designed with long sleeves and a scoop neckline finished with Venice lace. The bouffant skirt, held wide by hoops, ended in a short train.

—George Grant Photograph.

MRS. THEODORE C. SALVETER JR.

The bride chose a fingertip illusion veil held to a crown of seed pearls and carried white Fuji chrysanthemums and pale yellow sweetheart roses.

Miss Arlene Delores Yadon, Kansas City, Mo., was maid of honor, Miss Mary Ellen Downen, sister of the bride, and Miss Barbara Dee Boulware were bridesmaids.

Mr. Salveter, son of Mrs. Nelda Salveter, 584 Summit avenue, Webster Groves, had James Singer as best man. His brother, Charles Robert Salveter, and Ralph Dickenson, Kansas City, were ushers.

The bride, a graduate of Webster Groves High School, attended Drury College and became a member of Kappa Delta sorority. Mr. Salveter, a graduate of The Principia, also attended Drury College where his fraternity was Sigma Phi Epsilon. After a short wedding trip he and his bride will live in Webster Groves. He will enter St. Louis University School of Law this fall.

Inaugural Ball January, 1969

At the Inaugural Ball in Jefferson City

Representative and Mrs. Ted Salveter

Freshman Personalities of the Week

This weeks male feature spotlight falls on Larry Warner, Sigma Nu pledge from Shawnee Mission, Kansas. Larry is 17 years old, stands 5 feet, 10 inches tall, "and weighs 170 pounds; he has black hair and blue eyes.

At Shawnee Mission High School Larry played football for two years and basketball for one. He says he likes to participate in any and all kinds of s p o r t s though.

Larry doesn't have a hobby unless it's keeping track of his car. It seems as though it never has the necessary parts to keep it running. He has no favorite tune, but likes any rhythm and blue music.

When asked what he likes about Drury Larry replied, "I like the smallness of the school and the friendliness of all the students."

Sharon Downen from Webster Groves is the freshman girl reflected in our **Mirror** this week. Sharon who is 5 feet, 6 inches tall, has blonde hair and green eyes and a charming personality.

She attended Webster Groves High School where she was very active in the Pep Club, Spanish Club, Glee Club and Vespers.

Though her jewelry collection boasts a Kappa Delta pledge pin we can not overlook Skip Salveter's Sigma Phi Epsilon pin which Sharon tells us is her prize possession.

When she isn't studying (teachers please take note) or with Skip, Sharon enjoys knitting argyles or listening to any of Jack Gleason's records.

This 17-year-old has alread decided on a vocation when she leaves Drury. Sharon wants to be a teacher and says she'll have a composite major of Education and Spanish.

Sharon says she just loves Drury and likes the friendly atmosphere among the students and faculty.

Queen, Joe College Candidates Are Chosen

Candidates for Sou'wester Queen and Joe College were chosen recently by the various social organizations.

Those nominated for Queen and the groups sponsoring them are Virginia Miller, Independent Student Association; Florence Snidow, Sigma Nu; Jeanne Bender, Lambda Chi and Sharon Downen, Sigma Phi Epsilon. The Kappa Alpha choice has not been announced.

Joe College will be one of the following: Bob Hansen, the Tri Delta nominee; John Tutt, Kappa Delta; Rodger Parker, ISA; Charles Crosby, Pi Beta Phi; Max Jenkins, Alpha Phi; and Ron Rucker, Zeta Tau Alpha.

Joe College, to be selected by popular vote of all Drury girls, is supposed to be the ideal college man on the campus. The Sou'wester Queen will be chosen by a well-known person in the entertainment field who will be sent photographs of each candidate.

O.K. Joe Girl   *Miss Sharon Downen*

Kappa Delta sorority member Sharon Downen has been chosen the eleventh Don Sothern O.K. Joe Girl.

The nineteen-year old elementary education major is serving her sorority as corresponding secretary, is a member of the Spanish Club, and has worked in the library as an assistant. She's from Webster Groves, Mo.

Sharon's plans for the near future include a trip to Mexico with the Spanish class over the Easter vacation and a late summer wedding.

Don Sothern Studio

327 E. WALNUT   **PH. 6-0987**

1957

71

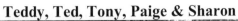

Teddy, Ted, Tony, Paige & Sharon

CHAPTER TWELVE

THEODORE CLIFTON SALVETER IV

My first born can be found in all the books I have written. He is fifty-seven now and continues to amaze me.

His strength, intellect, and deep devotion to his family and profession as an engineer are remarkable. Unlike me and his uncle Charles, "Good enough" is not in his vocabulary. Whatever he sets out to do must be done right. I suppose that's required in engineering or science. I could fudge a little with the law which is rarely exact.

Ted was born on October 25, 1960 in St. Johns Hospital, Springfield, Missouri. He was followed by his brother Philip Anthony Salveter on May 1, 1963, and his sister Paige Allison Salveter on January 6, 1967.

The kids all went to Roundtree Elementary, Jarrett Junior High, and Parkview High School. Ted did one year of kindergarten at Sunshine Elementary.

Testing indicated Ted would be a good engineer so when he graduated from Parkview in 1979 he was off to Rolla to get a Geological Engineering degree. Rolla, or Missouri S & T as it is now called, is one of the top schools in the nation.

Why geological engineering? Because that was one of the hottest degrees going due to the oil boom. By the time he graduated in 1983 the bang had gone out of the boom. Therefore, IV headed off to Columbia and Missouri U to pursue a masters in Civil Engineering with an emphasis on environmental engineering.

The masters was almost complete when he was offered a job in Little rock to work for the State. He took it and became an expert in Federal grants and Superfund projects.

One day he called me and said he had been offered a job with McLarin-Hart Consulting Engineers who were about to open a huge office in Springfield. I urged him to take it so he would be home.

On January 13, 1990 he married Lisa Stark in Little Rock, a girl he had met at the State Capitol. Then he moved back to Springfield with Lisa and her daughter Rachael. He adopted Rachael and we became instant grandparents. They moved to 759 S. Forest. That February we had a reception for them at our house at 1635 E. Delmar. Tony was practicing law then with Skook, Hardy, & Bacon in Kansas City. He came home to celebrate with big brother and the new family. It was the last time we saw him alive.

On March 6, 1990 Tony had a fatal accident at Troost and Gregory in Kansas City. He was going home after playing a basketball game. Tony's death was something we never got over.

Brennon Anthony Salveter, was born in St. Johns Hospital on June 14, 1991. Brennon "Anthony" is named after his Uncle Tony and so is his son Henry "Anthony" born March 17, 2014. Hard to believe my son is a grandfather.

Ted and Lisa divorced in 1998 in Greene County, Missouri.

He married Arlene Glad on the 30th day of June, 2006. They had no children. Rachael adopted Claire Salveter. She was born April 25, 2011. Rachael also had another daughter, Emilia Salveter Rose was born March 9, 2017 in Augusta, Georgia. "Millie's" father is Trey Enfinger, III. Rachael graduated from Willard High School and attended Drury University and Arkansas University. She was a Tri Delta. One of her jobs was Events Coordinator for Jerry Jones and the Dallas Cowboys. She continues to have similar jobs.

Brennon married Stephanie on August 11, 2013. They live in Nixa, Missouri. He has outgrown all of us and must be 6'3" or so. He graduated from Nixa High School. He is a good athlete in basketball, baseball and soccer. Stephanie is the greatest. A great wife and mother. She grew up in Stone County and graduated from Galena High School.

One of McLarin's clients was Springfield City Utilities. Ted did environmental work for them. He traveled around the country for

McLarin and could possibly be relocated to another city. He called me one day to tell me City Utilities had offered him an in house engineering position. To keep him home I said, "Take it!"

He has done a marvelous job for them. Arlene also works for C.U. As if I didn't feel old enough, they are talking about retirement. "Holy Cow!"

In Junior High at Jarrett Ted played football and basketball. In basketball they were undefeated champs in 7th and 8th grade. At Parkview he played football, basketball and tennis. He also wrestled his freshman year. Of course he played Mitey Mite football and Little League baseball. He has done lots of camping and hiking.

In 1986 or so he and I did an eight day backpacking in the Smokey Mountains. It was quite an adventure and I realized what a strong and competent man my son had become. We also did some backpacking in the Arkansas Boston Mountains. It was there that I realized the wilderness was dangerous. Perhaps I was too old to do it anymore. After a few close calls Ted decided he wasn't taking his dad on anymore of them. Probably a good thing, but great memories.

He now spends a lot of time on his ten acre farm near Bois D'arc. It sits right in the middle of the Missouri Conservation area. He will be rehabbing all the old buildings, barns, etc forever. He and Arlene are a good team.

He has asked me many times if anyone "fact checks" my books or articles. I guess he will have to check this one.

ARLENE ANN SALVETER

Arlene Ann Salveter was born February 9, 1961 in St. Luke's Hospital, Milwaukee, WI. She was raised Catholic by her parents Richard M. and Florence Kwasinski. She graduated from Coronado High school in Scottsdale, Arizona in 1979. She attended a community college in Scottsdale and Arizona State. She completed her education at Drury University in 2008 with a degree in Business Management Summa Cum Laude. She had no children of her own, but is a great step-mother to Brennon and step-grandmother to Henry.

She also is employed at City Utilities and works with computers and business systems, all of which I do not understand. She loves cats and used to play golf. She has a fantastic garden each year.

Ted and Arlene are avid Cardinal Baseball fans and spent their honeymoon and all anniversaries at Cardinal baseball games in St. Louis. She loves cats, and tolerates dogs.

She is a great addition to our family and a terrific daughter-in-law.

Bren, Ted, Rachael & Sharon Salveter
1998

Rachael & Ted Salveter
April, 1991

Bren, Ted & Rachael Salveter
June 16, 2017

Rachael & Ted Salveter
April 1991

Brennon, Ted IV, Ted III & Henry Salveter – Ellie Mae
Four Generations - Meramec River October 21, 2017

Andy Brez, Ted, Henry, Brennon & Teddy Salveter
Bagnell Dam – October 19, 2016

Ted, Paige, Arlene, Teddy Salveter
Father's Day – Kansas City – June 16, 2016

Claire, Ted & Henry Salveter
June 14, 2014

Henry & Ted Salveter III
Bagnell Dam
October 9, 2016

Stephanie, Henry & Brennon Salveter
Christmas - 2017

Henry
2017

Arlene, Becky, Charles, Teddy, Amy, Andy Brez & Paige Salveter
Christmas Brunch 2016 – Bois D'Ark

**Ted, Tony &
Teddy Salveter**
Theodore
Salveter's Grave
St. Charles Old
City Cemetery
1970

**Uncle Tom Downen &
Teddy Salveter**
1967

Tony & Teddy Salveter
Dental Hygiene
1967

**Ted, Teddy &
Tony Salveter**
Baseball Lesson
1968

Tony & Teddy
Brothers
1964

CHAPTER THIRTEEN

PAIGE ALLISON SALVETER

Like some of the others, Paige is in my books. Those should be read. She was born in St. Johns Hospital on January 6, 1967.

The truth is that Sharon and I had carefully planned for Teddy and Tony, but Paige was a surprise baby.

At least for me.

Long after Paige was an adult Sharon told me that she had planned for her. Apparently Sharon went off her birth control. She had no problem getting me to do my part. The surprise was a little shocking to me at the time.

How thankful I am that Sharon did it. I can't imagine life without my little girl. She has been a true blessing.

Three great kids!

Paige has boundless energy and there is never a dull moment when she is around. She is still involved heavily in tennis as player and coach. After many marketing jobs with Purina, various ad firms, Block Commercial Real Estate, American Century Investments, and now the NAIA, she still somehow manages to keep a lot of balls in the air.

She introduced her husband Andy Brez to tennis and he has become addicted to it too. They are both on many Kansas City Club teams and World Team Tennis. She had a good run as the Varsity Women's Tennis coach at Shawnee Mission West where they won a couple of Kansas State Championships. She was number one player at Parkview High school, and William Jewel College where she won several conference championships.

I just wish that my knees hadn't given out so we could still play. We had our own court at 1635 E. Delmar and the whole family was pretty good.

Paige is a dog lover and has had many. It is very sad when they die. They become like family. Currently she has two Labradoodles, Esty and Tulah. Paige had no children so the dogs are like her kids. She does have two step children, Cody and Sophie Brez.

Paige started out in social work and has a degree from William Jewell in Recreational Therapy. She also has a degree in Therapeutic Recreation from Missouri State University. With those degrees she did her internship at Shoal Creek Mental Hospital and got a job with Charter Mental Hospital, both in Austin, Texas.

We were thrilled when she got a job at Epworth Children's Home in Webster Groves, Missouri. Sharon and I had both grown up there. Paige was later hired by the Webster Hills Methodist Church to run a new recreational Center. It was quite a place.

One day she called me to say that she wasn't making much money. I reminded her that she worked for a rich church but a church nonetheless, and she shouldn't expect to get rich doing it. I never forgot her words. "Well, in that case, I'll just have to go corporate!"

That was her plan and she pursued it to the T. She got a job in the marketing department at Purina's International headquarters in St. Louis. Along the way to going "corporate" she earned an MBA from Webster University and also a Masters in Education. Four degrees plus numerous hours at other schools. I am sure she has more collegiate hours than anyone else and holds the world record.

She is now happily employed as the Vice President for Marketing for the NAIA at its national headquarters in Kansas City. The job is perfect for her sports and academic background. I couldn't be more proud.

Becky's youngest child is Bud Hogan. He and Paige were great friends and in the same class at Jarrett and Parkview high school. It is interesting to see how life has thrown Becky and I together and our kids as well. Teddy and Kim Hogan Chaffin were also in the same class as were Tony and Crista Hogan.

It's all quite amazing.

Ted & Paige Salveter
Lake of the Ozarks
October 9, 2016

Ted & Paige Salveter
Farm – Halltown – 2015

Ted, Paige & Rachael Salveter
Rep. Mel Hancock's Office
Washington DC

Paige Salveter

Paige Salveter has learned a lot since she graduated from Parkview High School in 1985. Now 23 years old and a 1989 graduate of William Jewell College, she has come to realize that one's plans and ambitions can and do change drastically.

"My major in college at first was nursing," she explained. But after working toward that goal for three years, she began to realize that she wanted to change her career path—but also that she still wanted to enter a field in which she can work with people.

At first, she opted for a degree in exercise physiology. But in her fourth year at William Jewell, during an internship in cardiac rehabilitation and exercise, she decided instead to work on a degree in recreation therapy and fitness management.

During that time, in addition to working with cardiac patients, she had some experience with children who were developmentally delayed. "I talked with a lady about a job, because I was going to graduate in December," Salveter said. "She asked if I was certified in therapeutic recreation. When I said I wasn't, she told me that Southwest Missouri State University has a really good program."

After talking with Gary Thompson, now her advisor at SMSU, she found that she could probably finish the work in two semesters and an internship. Last January she began taking the classes. But in the meantime, she wanted a job to help with expenses.

"I got this job with Lakes Country Rehabilitation Center," she said, referring to the place where she has worked for the past several months. Certification was not required, so she was able to take the job and gain some experience in the field.

She works with adult men and women at the center who are drug and alcohol abusers. "I just love my job," Salveter said.

Through that job, she has learned a lot about the field and had valuable experience. In addition, she is finishing up her work at SMSU.

Now her plans once again have taken a new turn. "I'm moving to Austin, Texas, a couple of days after Christmas," she explained. "I'll do an internship there at Shoal Creek Hospital, which is a mental health facility.

"I will be working with adolescents and also in their chemical dependency unit," she said, adding, "That will be a 10-week internship—and after that, they have an opening and I'm hoping that maybe I can get on there permanently. Also, after you do the internship there, you take a national certification examination."

What is recreation therapy? How does a staff work with drug and alcohol dependency?

"Rec therapy can be used with a lot of different populations, like mentally retarded persons or children who are developmentally disabled or the handicapped, in addition to drug and alcohol abuse," she explained.

Salveter said that many people have the wrong concept of what is done with recreation therapy. "They may think that all we do is play volleyball or take them to play tennis, but in our training we learn to work with leisure counseling, documentation of how the clients reacted to the particular therapy and what their general attitude was during the experience of interacting with the group," Salveter said.

Some of the people she works with don't know any way to use leisure time except to drink alcohol or take drugs, she explained. Her task is to show them other, more acceptable and better outlets for their time or energy.

"We try to build up their self-esteem, because it is real low. We show them different activities. We take them to the park to play tennis or basketball. Or we do a lot of cultural things—like take them to the art museum, or to watch dress rehearsals at Landers Theatre, or we may make a tour of the library or go to the zoo."

A lot of the clients are very intelligent, she explained, but their abilities are constantly being eroded by alcohol and drugs. Others have had little background of knowledge or experiences. The clients are not prisoners and they are not forced to take part in the rehabilitation program. The only time it's forced is in a women's program, where the women live, eat and stay at the facility, if their parole officer says it's either stay in the program or go back to jail, she said. In a men's program, the men work all day and then come to a half-way house in the evening and stay there for the night. Some of these men come because they want to, and some because they are required to, she explained.

"I love the work, but it's very frustrating sometimes, because these people are very unmotivated," Salveter said.

Due to the great amount of drug and alcohol abuse now present in our society, Salveter said there is an increasing demand for people trained as recreational therapists. "Our whole society has become very unmotivated due to video games and all of the electronics," she added.

Paige Salveter is grateful to her parents, Ted and Sharon Salveter, for the solid background of values and experiences they provided for her.

She wants to go to Austin, get the experience of a new work situation and have the opportunity to see another part of the world.

Nine months ago, her brother, Tony, was killed in an automobile accident in Kansas City. "One thing I have learned from his death is that you have to enjoy life now," she said.

"You don't know when it's going to be taken from you."

December 1990

CHAPTER FOURTEEN

PHILIP ANTHONY SALVETER

Tony was born on May 1, 1963 and died on March 8, 1990 as a result of a vehicular accident in Kansas City, Missouri. He was 26 years old and working at Shook, Hardy and Bacon in the Business Litigation Section. He was not married but was in a serious relationship.

His death was a severe blow to me and our family. I wrote a book about him and his life called "His Wonderful Life'. It's a take of the Christmas movie with Jimmy Steward called "It's a Wonderful Life". That was his favorite movie.

He had a wonderful education starting with grade school at Roundtree Elementary, Jarrett Junior High and Parkview High School where he graduated in 1981. From there he went to William Jewell College and graduated Summa Cum Laude in 1985. His degrees were in Business and Psychology. From there he went to The Missouri University School of Law and graduated in 1988. He also attended Oxford University in 1984 at Regents College. He was a straight A student.

Tony had many friends and beside his many accomplishment he had a winning charm and personality. He is missed by all I am sure. Some of his lifelong friends, he grew up with, are Dr. Tom Essman, Dr. Bob Thurman, Dr. Ed Hogan and Debbie Mallonie Hart. College and law school friends plus chums at Shook.

He was a member of the University Heights Baptist Church where he was baptized and where his funeral was held. He lays at rest in Maple Park Cemetery with his grandfather and mother.

With all he had to offer, there is no telling what his accomplishments might have been. Look around and you will see that life isn't always fair. I suspect my assessment of all that would be much more severe.

In February of 1990 Tony came home for a party we were having to introduce Teddy's new wife to our friends. That was the last time we saw him alive except briefly at St. Joseph's Hospital.

He loved his uncle Charles, and on his way home he stopped to see him at a farm. After they visited a while, and one of his big bear hugs, he drove off back to KC as Charlie saw him slowly disappear.

We all miss him so.

Tony was very athletic and was 6'1" and 190 pounds at the time of his death. He was a lifelong tennis player. His family had their own court. He played for Parkview all four years.

He played Mitey Mite football from first grade through sixth. At Jarrett he played football and basketball. At Parkview, besides tennis, he was a debater, a member of the band and played the soprano saxophone in the jazz band.

He also appeared in plays and musicals including Brigadoon as Harry Beaton. He loved to sing and was a 4 year member of the choir.

At WJC he was a member of Phi Gamma Delta and played all sports for his fraternity. At Oxford he rowed 8s for Regents and rowed in the 1984 Oxford Torpids. He also played on the tennis team there and his first match was against the Crown Prince of Japan.

Somehow he managed to also play basketball for Regents and we were in England and got to see him play for the championship. His time at Oxford and Europe was probably his most cherished life experience.

He never stopped playing and while driving home from a league basketball game on March 6, 1990 his accident happened. His Life was amazingly full and ended far too soon.

2B Monday, March 12, 1990

People came first for

By Michelle Beth Katzenell
The News-Leader

For Philip Anthony Salveter, people and relationships took precedence over personal success.

But the 26-year-old former Springfieldian, called "Tony" by friends and family, had a list of accomplishments that was longer than that of many people his age.

Today family and friends will say goodbye to Salveter at his funeral in University Heights Baptist Church in Springfield. But they won't be letting go of their memories.

Salveter died Thursday from injuries suffered in an automobile accident in Kansas City, where he lived and worked as an attorney.

"He was always incredibly sensitive about life and the people around him," said Tom Essman, who has been best friends with Salveter since they were 4. "Human relationships — family and friends — were most important, and everything else was secondary."

Essman, 26, now is practicing ophthalmology in Ann Arbor, Mich., at the University of Michigan.

A flood of memories fills Essman's mind when asked about the 22 years he shared with Salveter: playing tennis, playing bas-

OZARKS   The News-Leader

former Springfieldian, friends say

ketball in Salveter's garage, sleeping in a tree house and staying up all night talking in a screened-in porch.

"You always knew whatever happened, he'd always be there for you," Essman said.

Essman said he'll always be able to picture the "cheesy smile" or hear the "chimpanzee yell" that Salveter used to entertain his friends "when he felt the mood."

Alison Blessing, who went to William Jewell College, Liberty, and University of Missouri-Columbia Law School with Salveter, also is in Springfield to say goodbye. She lives in Kansas City where she also practices law.

When Blessing learned of Salveter's death, her mind raced back to a day in 1983 in England where the two also studied together at Oxford University.

"One day we took a day trip to London. It was a really nice out, and we spent the whole day walking through parks," Blessing recalled.

Walking, talking, and listening were among Salveter's greatest assets, his friends agreed. But he's also recognized as a person who has attained success professionally.

In addition to being a member of the Missouri Bar Association and American Bar Association, he was a member of the

Order of the Coif and editor of the Law Review at the University of Missouri-Columbia Law School. He graduated Summa Cum Laude from William Jewell in 1984.

Salveter's only dream that he hadn't accomplished was having a family of his own, friends said. It was his parents — Ted and Sharon Salveter of Springfield — whom he looked to for help in achieving his other goals.

"I think about what a great relationship he had with his parents," Essman said. "He always idolized his father. And I think that was one of the things that shaped him most."

Tony Salveter

KANSAS CITY — Philip Anthony Salveter, 26, Kansas City, died at 12:30 a.m. Thursday March 8, 1990, in St. Joseph Hospital, Kansas City, from injuries sustained in an auto accident on March 6, 1990.

He was born May 1, 1963, in Springfield. He was a 1981 graduate of Parkview High School, a graduate of William Jewell College and a 1988 graduate of the University of Missouri School of Law. He also attended Oxford University in England. He was an honor student and graduated Summa Cum Laude from William Jewell. In law school he was a member of the Order of the Coif and editor of the Law Review. He was an attorney with Schook, Hardy, and Bacon in Kansas City, working in the Business Litigation Department. He was a member of the Kansas City Bar Association, Missouri Bar Association, and American Bar Association. He was an avid sportsman and participated in basketball, volleyball, softball, and tennis. He was a member of University Heights Baptist Church in Springfield.

He is survived by his parents, Ted and Sharon Salveter; one brother, Ted Salveter, IV; one sister, Paige Salveter; grandfather, Ted Salveter Sr. and grandmother, Miriam Donner, all of Springfield; his uncles, Charles Salveter, Judge Auther McConnell, and Robert Biesinger; aunts, Karen Salveter, Pat Biesinger, and Mary McConnell.

He will be missed by his friends and classmates.

Services will be at 1 p.m. Monday, March 12, 1990, in University Heights Baptist Church with Dr. Michael Olmsted, Dr. Doug Devel, and Dr. Jerry Sandidge officiating. Burial will be in Maple Park Cemetery under direction of Klingner Mortuary.

Visitation will be from 4 to 6 p.m. Sunday in Klingner Chapel.

The family request that in leiu of flowers, your love may be expressed by donations to William Jewell College, Liberty, Mo., Tony Salveter Scholarship Fund.

Attorney Tony Salveter
1990

Tony & Dr. Ed Hogan
St. Stephens, Venice – August 1988

Tony & Dr. Ed Hogan
Poland – August 1988

Tony and Grandma Downen
1978

Tony and Grandma Downen
William Jewell College
1988

Tony & Dad
1988

Grandma Downen, Uncle Charles & Tony Salveter
1988

CHAPTER FIFTEEN

REBECCA KRUSE HOGAN (SALVETER)

Becky and I were married on May 31st, 2011 at Christ Episcopal Church in Springfield Missouri. We had both lost our spouses, Sharon Lee Salveter and Jack E. Hogan. She was so attached to the name Hogan that she kept it. I married an independent, beautiful and liberated woman.

Becky was born on September 14, 1940 in Springfield. She lost her parents at an early age, and her brother Bud Kruse a little later. She has three children; Kim Chaffin, Crista Hogan, and Bud Hogan. She has eight grandchildren and two great grandchildren. Beck and Jack started Hogan Title. It is now run by Kim, Bud and Keith. She graduated from Greenwood in 1958 and went there all thirteen years.

We both enjoy golf and are members at Hickory Hills. I gave up my membership at Twin Oaks after we were married. She routinely beats me at the game of golf. We are both interested in physical fitness and Becky is an excellent swimmer. I challenged her to race, but gracefully backed out when I saw her swim.

We have an extremely active social life and enjoy dances where we can show the youngsters how it's done. We also like to travel, but she more than me. I'm pretty much a short trip guy, but she goes over both oceans. I take care of the dog and the house when that happens.

We share a marriage in our "golden years". A strange name for those of us who know it's not always golden. Finding love and companionship at our age is a special thing. We try not to take it for granted. Our kids all seem to be happy about our marriage and our happiness. That is a blessing. I know I'm quite lucky, I hope she feels that way, too.

How it all works out remains to be seen. I'm betting on terrific. Becky's grandchildren are Sam, Ross and Anabelle Chaffin, Jack and Nick Hogan, Rebecca, Theo and Claude Shuler, and the two great grandchildren, Soren and Margot Carroll. This makes me have a lot of "steps." Kim, Crista, Sam, Ross and probably Anabelle are all lawyers.

Beck has many long term friends and they are very loyal to each other. Of interest are the female classmates from Greenwood, who also were there the entire thirteen years. They manage to gather together somewhere special twice a year. I believe that is very unique, and quite remarkable.

I should not fail to mention she is very fond of wine, along with her golfing buddies. Besides drinking it, she knows a lot about it.

We belong to two wine clubs. Maybe being Episcopalian has something to do with it. That communion thing you know. I know wine is red or white and can come in a jug.

Becky Hogan & Ted Salveter
50th SLU Law Reunion
September 25, 2010

Becky Hogan & Ted Salveter
Phoenix, Arizona
February 26, 2011

Becky and Ted's Wedding

Kim Chaffin, Kay Charles, Becky Hogan
Ted & Charles Salveter & Crista Hogan
Christ Church – May 31, 2011

Bud Hogan & Paige Salveter
2015
Sam Chaffin, Ted & Kim Chaffin

Christmas – 2015

Steph Salveter, Becky Hogan, Paige Salveter, Arlene Salveter
Toolah & Ellie Mae
Lake of the Ozarks
October 9, 2016

CHAPTER SIXTEEN

THE FUTURE

I leave it to others in my family to finish our story. Of course the story is never finished and future generations keep it going.

What I have attempted here is only a beginning. There is so much more that can be and should be said.

Who will do it?

My brother Charles knows much more than I. Maybe he will. If I'm still around I will enjoy reading what they write.

It is true that I am the only one so far to write about anything. I believe it was worthwhile, for me and for others.

Someday I'll ask my great grandson Henry Anthony Salveter what he thinks.

I wonder what his answer will be.

That will be an interesting day.

EPILOGUE

This book and the others I have written have been trips down "memory Lane" for me. What I remember and how I remembered are curious things indeed.

Studies show that maybe what we remember is not at all that accurate. It is sad for me to think I got some parts wrong, especially if it's a part I like or am comfortable with.

The song "The Way We Were" from the movie "The Way We Were", and beautifully sung by Barbara Streisand, speaks to this conundrum.

Memories light the corners of my mind
Misty water-colored memories of the way we were
Scattered pictures of the smiles we left behind
Smiles we gave to one another for the way we were

Can it be that it was all so simple then
Or has time rewritten every line
If we had the chance to do it all again
Tell me, would we?
Could we?

Memories may be beautiful and yet
What's too painful to remember
We simply choose to forget
So it's the laughter we will remember
Whenever we remember
The way we were
The way we were

Was it all perfect? Of course not. Is it comforting to remember the good? Of course. The bad gets pushed down into our sub-conscientious, maybe forever.

I can only deal with my memories. For those who have gone on I wonder what they would think, how they would remember.

A problem can arise if you remember one in your past as

perfect, when they were not. Someone in your present may be unfairly compared to a ghost that never existed. To a time that never was.

Maybe that's why the 'Make America Great Again" movement is wrong-headed. When was America ever great? What made it great? Was it a time you remember or a time someone told you about? It gets tricky.

What are your memories and what are you going to do about them? Will you share them or take them with you? I hope you share.

Ted Salveter III

ABOUT THE AUTHOR

Ted C. Salveter, III is a retired lawyer living in Springfield, Missouri. He grew up in Webster Groves in the St. Louis area during the 40's and 50's. He holds a degree in Psychology with a minor in English from Drury University, and a J.D. from St. Louis' University School of Law.

He has taught law and political science at Drury and Missouri State University. He was elected to the Springfield School Board and the Missouri Legislature

His other books are "His Wonderful Life" about his son Tony who died in 1990; "The Accidental Lawyer" an autobiography; and "The Fairytale Princess" about his wife Sharon who died in 2010.

Ethnicity estimate for ted salveter

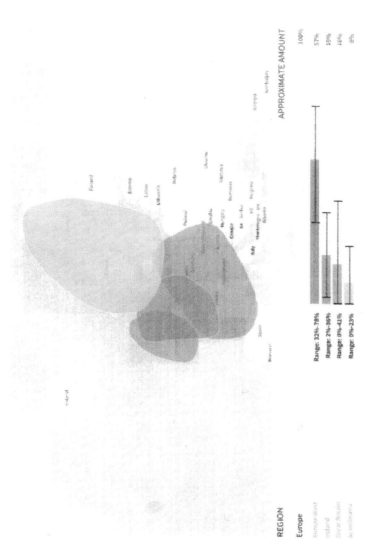

REGION

Europe

	APPROXIMATE AMOUNT
Europe West	57%
Ireland	15%
Great Britain	16%
Scandinavia	0%

Range: 32%-78%
Range: 2%-36%
Range: 0%-42%
Range: 0%-23%

18872418R00064

Made in the USA
Middletown, DE
09 December 2018